OUT ON A
Limerick

BENNETT CERF'S

OUT ON A

With
Illustrations
by
Saxon

Art from hardcover edition.

Limerick

A Collection of over 300 of the
World's Best Printable Limericks

Assembled, Revised, Dry-cleaned,
and Annotated by Mister Cerf

PERENNIAL LIBRARY

Harper & Row, Publishers, New York
Cambridge, Philadelphia, San Francisco, Washington
London, Mexico City, São Paulo, Singapore, Sydney

About one-third of the limericks in this volume originally appeared in the author's "Cerfboard" column in *This Week* magazine.

A hardcover edition of this book was originally published in 1960 by Harper & Brothers.

First PERENNIAL LIBRARY edition published 1987.

Library of Congress Cataloging-in-Publication Data

Bennett Cerf's out on a limerick.

  Reprint. Originally published: New York : Harper, 1960.
  1. Limericks. I. Cerf, Bennett, 1898–1971.
II. Title: Out on a limerick.
PN6231.L5B44   1987   821'.07'08   87-45322
ISBN 0-06-091451-3 (pbk.)

---

87 88 89 90 91 **MPC** 10 9 8 7 6 5 4 3 2 1

There is a young lady from Fife,
Whom I never have seen in my life.
  So the devil with her;
  Instead I prefer
To dedicate this to my wife.

CONTENTS

INTRODUCTION

THE ORIGIN of the limerick form is shrouded in obscurity, but there is no doubt whatever of the identity of the man who made it universally popular. His name was Edward Lear, artist and humorist, and his *Book of Nonsense,* published in London in 1846, initiated a vogue that spread more quickly than anagrams and bustles.

Nobody was more dismayed by this development than Edward Lear himself, who boarded a steamer and fled to Greece to escape the plague of limericks he had started. The first night at sea, the captain sought him out and declared, "Mr. Lear, it's an honor to have you aboard. I'd like your opinion of a couple of limericks I dashed off in my quarters this afternoon. . . ."

Lear insisted to the end, but in vain, that he was not the *originator* of the limerick form. He even produced in evidence a limerick of sorts by *William Shakespeare!* The lines appear in Act 2, Scene 3, of *Othello,* and are sung by Iago:

> "And let me the canakin clink, clink;
> And let me the canakin clink.
>   A soldier's a man;
>   O, man's life's but a span,
> Why then, let a soldier drink."

Lear had aspired to be a landscape painter, and produced a portfolio of drawings of various species of birds that has been compared favorably to Audubon's. When he discovered, therefore, that his fame would rest on the composition of a book of *limericks,* his consternation is understandable. As Douglas Reed put it:

> A goddess capricious is Fame.
> You may strive to make noted your name.
>   But she either neglects you
>   Or coolly selects you
> For laurels distinct from your aim!

Edward Lear's limericks are elementary in comparison with today's more intricate form. They conclude for the most part with a "lazy" last line—a mere repetition of the first line. It remained for recognized poets, men of high station, and an enthusiastic general public to refine—if that is the word—the form. Soon limericks boasted a definite story line, not to mention atrocious puns, abbreviations, trick spellings—and obscenity.

For examples of the depths of depravity to which some fashioners of limericks descended, the reader is referred to a collection made and published surreptitiously in Florence, Italy, by Norman Douglas, distinguished author of *South Wind*. I spent hours, as a matter of fact, cleaning up a few of Douglas' cleverest concoctions so that I might include them in this volume. The true limerick connoisseur will be able to spot them from a distance of sixty paces.

George Bernard Shaw, a confirmed limerick aficionado, mourned that so many of them were unfit for publication. "They must be left," he wrote, "for oral tradition. Let us hope, however, that in the course of time, sufficient limericks which shall be decent as well as witty and ingenious may accumulate, and be collected in a volume that a reputable publisher dares touch!"

Herbert Langford Reed accepted Bernard Shaw's challenge. He produced in England, in 1924, a comprehensive and popular *Complete Limerick Book* and Carolyn Wells followed suit in America a year later. The cream of the Reed and Wells collections is included in this volume, supplemented by newer limericks, reprinted by permission, by such experts as Morris Bishop, Ogden Nash, Oliver Herford, Gelett Burgess, etc., plus a number of my own, and a hundred or so contributed for my "Cerfboard" column in *This Week* Magazine.

The limerick probably never again will achieve the vogue it enjoyed in Britain in the 1907-1908 season. A circulation-conscious London weekly initiated a "last line" contest which proved such an immediate success that competing journals hastily followed suit. Soon the rewards started multiplying (shades of the late-lamented big-money TV quiz programs!) and limerick contest winners were waltzing off with houses and lots, carriages and fancy equipage, and de-luxe round-the-world trips.

Each competitor was required to send a sixpence postal order as an entrance fee, and some idea of the scope of the craze may be gleaned from the fact that the monthly sale of sixpence money orders vaulted at the post offices in half a year from 700,000 to 11,400,000!

The contest that offered the most dazzling loot and accordingly the most entries (over 700,000) sought a last line for

> There was a young lady of Ryde
> Whose locks were consid'rably dyed.
> The hue of her hair
> Made everyone stare. . . .

The winning last line was " 'She's piebald, she'll die bald,' they cried."

One incorruptible newspaper editor in Ireland, it should be noted, remained haughtily aloof from the limerick commotion, and, to the disgust of his subscribers, refused to sponsor a prize-studded contest. This gentleman was none other than the editor of the Limerick *Times!* He always had resented the fact that his lively town, on the banks of the

River Shannon, just west of Tipperary, should by some appalling coincidence bear the same name as a verse form he abhorred. (Little credence today is given to the theory that the form was introduced first in Limerick by soldiers returned from wars on the Continent—about 1800.)

"Furthermore," wrote the editor, "I am sick unto death of obscure English towns that exist seemingly for the sole accommodation of these so-called limerick writers—and even sicker of their residents, all of whom suffer from physical deformities and spend their time dismembering relatives and attending fancy dress balls."

This selfsame editor met his severest test when a rash reader brought round a sheaf of limericks in person. Rudely rebuffed, the reader shouted, "I'll have you know I'm the featherweight champion of the Emerald Isle."

"Be you now?" replied the editor grimly. "Well, one more limerick out of you, my lad, and out you go—feathers and all!"

BENNETT CERF

Random House, New York
May, 1960

THE BIG TEN

The following ten limericks are the "aristocracy" of the breed—probably the most often quoted limericks of all time.

A wonderful bird is the pelican.
His mouth can hold more than his belican.
    He can take in his beak
    Enough food for a week.
I'm darned if I know how the helican.

The Reverend Henry Ward Beecher
Called a hen a most elegant creature.
    The hen, pleased with that,
    Laid an egg in his hat—
And thus did the hen reward Beecher.

               OLIVER WENDELL HOLMES

There was a young lady named Bright,
Whose speed was much faster than light.
   She went out one day
   In a relative way
And returned on the previous night.

There was a young man from the city
Who met what he thought was a kitty.
   He gave it a pat
   And said, "Nice little cat."
They buried his clothes, out of pity.

There was a young lady of Niger
Who smiled as she rode on a tiger.
   They returned from the ride
   With the lady inside
And the smile on the face of the tiger.

There was a young lady named Maud,
A sort of society fraud.
  In the parlor, 'tis told,
  She was distant and cold,
But on the veranda, my Gawd!

I wish that my room had a floor;
I don't so much care for a door,
    But this walking around
    Without touching the ground
Is getting to be quite a bore!

GELETT BURGESS

A doughty old person in Leeds
Rashly swallowed a packet of seeds.
  In a month, silly ass,
  He was covered with grass,
And he couldn't sit down for the weeds.

The bottle of perfume that Willie sent
Was highly displeasing to Millicent.
  Her thanks were so cold
  That they quarreled, I'm told,
Through that silly scent Willie sent Millicent.

God's plan made a hopeful beginning
But man spoiled his chances by sinning.
  We trust that the story
  Will end in God's glory
But, at present, the other side's winning.

LIMERICKS ABOUT LIMERICKS

Well, it's partly the shape of the thing
That gives the old limerick wing;
   These accordion pleats
   Full of airy conceits
Take it up like a kite on a string.

Pray search this wide land with a glimmer stick,
For there must be some lad at his primer quick,
   Who when pressed can supply
   A lot better than I
An acceptable rhyme scheme for limerick.

                  ELMO CALKINS

I'm bored to extinction with Harrison.
His lim'ricks and puns are embarrassin'.
   But I'm fond of the bum
   For, though dull as they come,
He makes me seem bright by comparison!

    The limerick is furtive and mean;
    You must keep her in close quarantine,
       Or she sneaks to the slums
       And promptly becomes
    Disorderly, drunk, and obscene.

                    MORRIS BISHOP

No matter how grouchy you're feeling,
You'll find that a limerick is healing.
   It grows in a wreath
   All around the front teeth,
Thus preserving the face from congealing.

    The limerick packs laughs anatomical
    Into space that is quite economical.
      But the good ones I've seen
      So seldom are clean,
    And the clean ones so seldom are comical!

TEN LIMERICKS BY EDWARD LEAR
("The Founder")

There was an old man with a beard
Who said, "It is just what I feared!
  Two owls and a hen,
  Four larks and a wren
Have all built their nests in my beard!"

There was an old lady of Chertsey,
Who made a remarkable curtsey:
  She twirled round and round
  Till she sank underground,
Which distressed all the people of Chertsey.

There was a young lady of Ryde
Whose shoe-strings were seldom untied.
   She purchased some clogs,
    And some small spotted dogs,
And frequently walked around Ryde.

There was an old man in a boat,
Who said, "I'm afloat! I'm afloat!"
   When they said, "No, you ain't,"
    He was ready to faint,
That unhappy old man in a boat.

There was an old man who said, "Hush!
I perceive a young bird in this bush!"
    When they said, "Is it small?"
    He replied, "Not at all!
It is four times as big as the bush!"

There was an old person of Cromer,
Who stood on one leg to read Homer.
    When he found he grew stiff,
    He jumped over the cliff,
Which concluded that person of Cromer.

There was an old man who supposed
That the street door was partially closed;
    But some very large rats
    Ate his coats and his hats,
While that futile old gentleman dozed.

There was an old man of Thermopylae
Who never did anything properly;
   But they said, "If you choose
   To boil eggs in your shoes,
You will have to get out of Thermopylae."

There was a young lady of Greenwich,
Whose garments were border'd with spinach,
   But a large spotty calf
   Bit her shawl quite in half,
Which alarmed that young lady of Greenwich.

There was a young lady of Clare
Who was hotly pursued by a bear.
   When she found she was tired
   She abruptly expired,
That unfortunate lady of Clare.

SOME LIMERICKS BY
FAMOUS MEN

There was a young maiden of Joppa
Who came a society cropper.
    She went off to Ostend
    With a gentleman friend
And the rest of the story's improper.

SAMUEL HOPKINS ADAMS

'Tis strange how the newspapers honor
A creature that's called prima donna.
    They say not a thing
    Of how she can sing
But write reams of the clothes she has on her.

EUGENE FIELD

There once lived a lad in Quebec
Who was buried in snow to his neck.
When asked, "Are you friz?"
He replied, "Yes, I iz,
But I hope it gets colder, by heck!"
RUDYARD KIPLING!!

A man hired by John Smith and Co.
Loudly declared that he'd tho.
Men that he saw
Dumping dirt near his store.
The drivers, therefore, didn't do.
MARK TWAIN

In New Orleans there dwelled a young Creole
Who when asked if her hair was all reole
Replied with a shrug,
"Just give it a tug
And decide by the way that I squeole."
V.P. ALBEN BARKLEY

There was an old man of the Cape
Who made himself garments of crepe.
  When asked, "Do they tear?"
  He replied, "Here and there,
But they're perfectly splendid for shape."
ROBERT LOUIS STEVENSON

There was an old man of St. Bees,
Who was stung in the arm by a wasp.
  When asked, "Does it hurt?"
  He replied, "No, it doesn't.
I'm so glad it wasn't a hornet."
  W. S. GILBERT (obviously fed up with limericks even
    then!)

There was a young man of Montrose
Who had pockets in none of his close.
  When asked by his lass
  Where he carried his brass,
He said, "Darling, I pay through the nose."
ARNOLD BENNETT

There was a young man from New York
Whose morals were lighter than cork:
  "Young chickens," said he,
  "Have no terrors for me:
The bird that *I* fear is the stork!"

HUGH GIBSON

As a beauty I am not a star.
There are others more handsome, by far.
  But my face, I don't mind it
  For I am behind it.
It's the people in front get the jar!

WOODROW WILSON

There was an old man of Khartoum
Who kept two ugly sheep in a room.
  "They remind me," he said,
  "Of two friends who are dead,"
But he never would tell us of whom.

DEAN INGE

To an artist a husband called Bicket
Said, "Turn your backside, and I'll kick it.
  You have painted my wife
  In the nude to the life.
Do you think for a moment that's cricket?"

JOHN GALSWORTHY

THE SOMEWHAT DIFFERENT SET

There once was a hermit named Green
Who grew so abnormally lean,
   And flat, and compressed,
   That his back touched his chest,
And sideways he couldn't be seen.

There's a young man who lives in Belsize
Who believes he is clever and wise.
   Why, what do you think?
   He saves gallons of ink
By merely not dotting his "i's"!

A patriot, living at Ewell,
Found his bonfire wanted more fuel,
   So he threw in Uncle James
   To heighten the flames,
A measure effective though cruel.

LANGFORD REED

31

There was a young lady of Malta
Who strangled her aunt with a halter.
   She said, "I won't bury her;
   She'll do for my terrier.
She should keep for a month if I salt her."

There was an old lady of Herm
Who tied bows on the tail of a worm.
   Said she, "You look festive
   But don't become restive:
You'll wiggle 'em off if you squirm."

A menagerie came to Cape Race
Where they loved the gorilla's grimace.
   It surprised them to learn
   That he *owned* the concern:
He was human, in spite of his face!

There was a fair maid whose maneuver
Was to get her portrait in the Louvre.
  But they sent it away
  On the very first day—
And it's now in a dive in Vancouver.

There was a young girl named Furness
Who invited a friend to play chess.
  But she'd lent half the pieces
  To one of her nieces
And couldn't recall the address.

There was a young man of Devizes
Whose ears were of different sizes.
  The one that was small
  Was of no use at all,
But the other won several prizes.

A sleeper from the Amazon
Put nighties of his gra'mazon—
  The reason: that
  He was too fat
To get his own pajamazon.

He died in attempting to swallow,
Which proves that, though fat, he was hollow,
  For in gasping for space
  He swallowed his face
And hadn't the courage to follow.

ROY CAMPBELL

I once took the bishop to tea;
It was just as I thought it would be.
  His rumblings abdominal
  Were simply phenomenal
And everyone thought it was me.

A jolly old Southern colonel
Has a humorous sense most infolonel.
   He amuses his folks
   By laughing at jokes
That appear in the *Ladies' Home Jolonel*.

From Number Nine, Penwiper Mews,
There is really abominable news:
   They've discovered a head
   In the box for the bread,
But nobody seems to know whose.

EDWARD GOREY

There was a young lady from Trent
Whose TV antenna got bent.
   The neighbors went crazy:
   Their screens all got hazy
For instead of receiving, she sent!

JOHN ETHERIDGE

The poor benighted Hindoo:
He does the best he kindoo.
   He sticks to caste
   From first to laste.
For pants he makes his skindoo.

A chemistry student named Boma
Produced such a potent aroma
   That half of the class
   Dropped dead, but alas,
The culprit received a diploma.

DON AUGUR

A fellow of little renown
Is becoming the talk of the town.
　His most recent quirk is
　To think he's a circus
Whereas he is only a clown.

AGNES PEARSON

There once was a lady named Harris
That nothing seemed apt to embarrass
　Till the bathsalts she shook
　In a tub that she took
Turned out to be plaster-of-Paris.

A skeleton once in Khartoum
Invited a ghost to his room.
　They spent the whole night
　In the eeriest fight
As to which should be frightened of whom.

There was a young lady of Stornaway
Who by walking had both her feet worn away.
　　Said she, "I won't mind
　　If only I find
That it's taken that terrible corn away."

There was a young lady of Crete
Who was so exceedingly neat,
　　When she got out of bed
　　She stood on her head
To make sure of not soiling her feet.

There was an old fellow of Eire
Who perpetually sat on the fire.
　　When asked, "Are you hot?"
　　He declared, "I am not.
I am Pat Winterbottom, Esquire."

A ghoulish old fellow in Kent
Encrusted his wife in cement.
　　He said with a sneer,
　　"I was careful, my dear,
To follow your natural bent."

MORRIS BISHOP

There was a young lady named Erskine
Who had a remarkably fair skin.
   When folks said to her, "Mabel,
   You look right smart in sable,"
She replied, "I look best in my bare skin."

There was a young lady of Tottenham
Whose manners—well, she had forgotten 'em.
   While at tea at the vicar's
   She took off her knickers
Explaining she felt much too hot in 'em!

There's a dowager near Sneden's Landing
Whose manners are bluff and commanding.
   It is one of her jests
   To trip up her guests,
For she hates to keep gentlemen standing.

MORRIS BISHOP

39

LOVE AND MARRIAGE

There once was a maid in Siam
Who said to her boy friend, Kiam,
   "If you kiss me, of course,
   You will have to use force,
But thank goodness you're stronger than I am."

There was a young lady of Lynn
Who was deep in original sin.
   When they said, "Do be good!"
   She said, "Would that I could!"
And straightway went at it again.

There's a vaporish maiden in Harrison
Who longed for the love of a Saracen.
　　But she had to confine her
　　Intent to a Shriner
Who suffers, I fear, by comparison.

MORRIS BISHOP

It's time to make love. Douse the glim.
The fireflies twinkle and dim.
　　The stars lean together
　　Like birds of a feather,
And the loin lies down with the limb!

CONRAD AIKEN

Wrote a swain to his gal in Saskatchewan:
"If you'll wear my ring, I'll dispatchewan
　　By parcel post when
　　In some five-and-ten
If the clerk turns his head I can snatchewan."

There once was a man not unique
In fancying himself quite a shique.
　　But the girls didn't fall
　　For this fellow at all
For he only made thirty a wique.

A young trapeze artist named Bract
Is faced by a very sad fact.
   Imagine his pain
   When, again and again,
He catches his wife in the act!

A lady there was in Antigua
Who said to her spouse, "What a pigua."
   He answered, "My queen,
   Is it manners you mean?
Or do you refer to my figua?"

A freshman from down in Laguna
Once fell in love with a tuna.
   The affair, although comic,
   Was so economic
He wished he had thought of it suna.

An earnest young teaching assistant
From the facts of the world was far distant.
  A girl in his section
  Made a discreet suggestion
Which would have caused him to flee if he listant.

A naughty old colonel in Butte
Had a habit his friends thought was cutte.
  He'd slip off to Spokane
  And proceed from the train
To a house of distinct ill reputte.

A near-sighted fellow named Walter
Led a glamorized lass to the altar.
  A beauty he thought her
  Till some soap and hot water
Made her look like the rock of Gibraltar.

She married a fellow named Leicester.
With triplets the Lord one day bleicester.
    Les looked at that trio
    And shrieked, "One, two, three, oh,
I wonder whatever posseicester?"

A dentist named Archibald Moss
Fell in love with the dainty Miss Ross,
    But he held in abhorrence
    Her Christian name, Florence,
So he renamed her his Dental Floss.

Concerning the bees and the flowers
In the fields and the gardens and bowers,
    You will note at a glance
    That their ways of romance
Haven't any resemblance to ours.

Said a fellow from North Philadelphia
To his girl, "When I saw ya, I fellphia.
    It was love at first sight,
    But 'twill last, honor bright,
Till the church bells are ringing a knellphia."

BERTON BRALEY

An impetuous swordsman from Parma
Was lovingly fondling a charma.
  Said the maiden demure,
   "You'll excuse me, I'm sure,
But I THINK you're still wearing your arma."

Said newlywed henpecked McLeod,
"I wish that two wives were aleod
   For I've found out that one
   Is a son-of-a-gun
And three, I've been told, is a creoud."
                  WILLIAM ENGEL

There was a young lady from Gloucester
Whose husband once thought he had loucester.
  But he found her that night
  In the icebox, locked tight.
We all had to help him defroucester.

45

A fellow they call Aloysius
Of his wife and a gent grew suspysius
    And as quick as a wink
    Found the two by a sink
But they only were doing the dysius.

MAX LIEF

Said a potentate gross and despotic,
"My tastes are more rich than exotic.
    I've always adored
    Making love in a Ford
Because I am auto-erotic."

MARY OWEN RANK

There was a young lady of Condover
Whose husband had ceased to be fond of her.
    He could not forget
    He had wooed a brunette
But peroxide had now made a blonde of her.

A maiden fair from Aberystwyth
Took some grain to the mill to make grystwyth.
    The miller's son Jack,
    With her arms round his back,
Pressed his own to the lips that she kystwyth.

There was a young lady in Eton
Whose figure had plenty of meat on.
    She said, "Marry me, dear,
    And you'll find that my rear
Is a nice place to warm your cold feet on."

There once was a maid with such graces
That her curves cried aloud for embraces.
    "You look," said McGee,
    "Like a million to me—
Invested in all the right places."

There was a young fellow named Hammer
Who had an unfortunate stammer.
    "The b-b-bane of my life,"
    Said he, "is m-my wife,
D-d-d-d-d-damn 'er!"

There was a young lady named Florence
Who for kissing expressed great abhorrence.
　　But when she'd been kissed,
　　And found what she'd missed,
She cried till the tears came in torrents.

There was a young lady named Stella
Fell in love with a bowlegged fella.
　　The venturesome chap
　　Let her sit on his lap
And she plummeted down to the cella.

An indolent vicar of Bray
His roses allowed to decay.
　　His wife, more alert,
　　Bought a powerful squirt,
And said to her spouse, "Let us spray."

There once was a maiden Circassian
Who was loved by a courtier of fashion.
　　When he vowed he adored her,
　　* * * * *,
(The asterisks indicate passion.)

There's a tiresome young man in Bay Shore:
When his fiancée cried, "I adore
  The beautiful sea!"
  He replied, "I agree
It's pretty, but what is it FOR?"

MORRIS BISHOP

A Mr. De Lyssa of Leigh
Started kissing his girl by the sea.
  "This can't be good kissing,"
  Said the girl. "I hear hissing."
Said De Lyssa, still kissing, "That's me."

There was a young man of Fort Blainey
Who proposed to a typist named Janey.
  Mourned his friends, "You can't win.
  She's as ugly as sin."
He explained, "But the day was so rainy!"

For hours my wife says "Goodbye"
And a marvel of patience am I.
　　I can bridle my passion
　　Through servants and fashion
But at mention of babies, I fly.

GELETT BURGESS

Said an ardent young bridegroom named Trask,
"I will grant any boon that you ask."
　　Said the bride, "Kiss me, dearie,
　　Until I grow weary,"
But he died of old age at the task.

CAROLYN WELLS

There was a young fellow from Fife
Who had a big row with his wife.
   He lost half his nose,
   Two thirds of his toes,
One ear, seven teeth—and his life.

Said a man to his spouse in East Sydenham,
"My best trousers! Now where have you hydenham?
   It is perfectly true
   They were not very new
But I foolishly left half a quidenham."

PUNCH

Said a fair-headed maiden of Klondike,
"Of you I'm exceedingly fond, Ike.
   To prove I adore you
   I'll dye, darling, for you
And be a brunette, not a blonde, Ike."

LANGFORD REED

A contemptuous matron in Shoreham
Behaved with extreme indecorum.
   She snapped a sarcastic
   And secret elastic
Throughout the community forum.

THE WORLD AROUND US

Animals

Said an ape as he swung by his tail
To his children, both female and male,
   "From your offspring, my dears,
   In a couple of years,
May evolve a professor at Yale!"

A lady from near Lake Louise
Declared she was bothered by fleas.
   She used gasoline
   And later was seen
Sailing over the hills and the trees.

A venerable dame in Nic'ragua
Had her back hair nipped off by a jaguar.
    The lady gasped, "Ah,"
    The jaguar, "Bah!
What a false, artificial old haguar."

Said a cat, as he playfully threw
His wife down a well in Peru,
    "Relax, dearest Dora,
    Please don't be angora;
I only was artesian you."

According to experts, the oyster
In its shell—or crustacean cloister—
    May frequently be
    Either he or a she
Or both, if it should be its choice ter.

BERTON BRALEY

A cat in despondency sighed
And resolved to commit suicide.
    She passed under the wheels
    Of eight automobiles
And under the ninth one she died.

A duck whom I happened to hear
Was complaining quite sadly, "Oh, dear!
    Our picnic's today
    But the weathermen say
That the skies will be sunny and clear."

A certain old maid in Cohoes
In despair taught her bird to propose;
    But the parrot, dejected,
    At being accepted,
Spoke some lines too profane to disclose.

There was a young man who was bitten
By twenty-two cats and a kitten.
    Cried he, "It is clear
    That my end is quite near.
Nonetheless I shall die like a Briton!"

Said an envious, erudite ermine,
"There's one thing I cannot determine:
   When a dame wears my coat
   She's a person of note;
When I wear it, I'm called only vermin."

    There was a sightseer named Sue
    Who saw a strange beast at the zoo.
       When she asked, "Is it old?"
       She was smilingly told,
    "It's not an old beast, but a gnu."

A mouse in her room woke Miss Dowd.
She was frightened, it must be allowed.
   Then a happy thought hit her:
   To scare off the critter,
She climbed down from her chair and meowed.

Books

A poetess luscious and trim
Indulged in a mighty strange whim:
   When composing a sonnet
   She affected a bonnet
But stripped herself bare for a hymn.

   A publisher once went to France
   In search of a tale of romance.
      A Parisian lady
      Told a story so shady
   That the publisher made an advance.

A bookworm from Kennebunk, Me.
Found pleasure in reading Monte.
   But he got little wallop
   From that Lolita trollop,
And Lady Chatterley's ways caused him pe.

An authoress armed with a skewer
Once hunted a hostile reviewer.
   "I'll teach him," she cried,
    "When I've punctured his hide,
To call my last novel too pure."

Twas a mariner ancient said, "Say,
Stick around, kid, and list to my lay.
   Shot a bird for a joke,
    Saw my shipmates all croak,
Now I give to the S.P.C.A."

F.P.A.

A student who lives up in Worcester
Is reading much more than he ucester.
   He's filled up his closet
    With reprints from Grosset
And acrostics from Simon and Shucester.

Said a booklover fellow in Siam,
"I frequently read Omar Khayyám.
    His morals depress
    But nevertheless
He is almost as clever as I am."

The fabulous wizard of Oz
Retired from business becoz
    What with up-to-date science
    To most of his clients
He wasn't the wiz that he woz.

Business

A merchant addressing a debtor
Set down in the course of his lebtor,
    "I choose to suppose
    A man knose what he ose
And the sooner he pays it the bedtor."

An extraordinary tailor in Kan.
Fashioned nothing but formal striped pan.
    When told that they'd sell
    If he made coats as well
He eventually came to his san.

My stenographer's notable glamour
Couldn't quite compensate for her gramour.
    She got me so ired
    That I told her, "You're fired!"
Now I wish she was back again, damour!

Annoying Miss Tillie McLush
Shopped early, avoiding the crush,
    Then brought everything back
    And demanded her jack
At the peak of the holiday rush.

JOSEPH S. NEWMAN

They've buried a salesman named Phipps.
He married on one of his trips
    A widow named Block,
    Then died of the shock
When he found there were five little chips.

As he filled up his order book pp.
He decided, "I want higher ww."
   So he struck for more pay
   But alas, now, they say,
He is sweeping out elephants' cc.

Collegiate

An imprudent coed in De Pauw
Committed a dreadful faux pas.
   She loosened a stay
   In her new décolleté
Exposing her je ne sais quoi.

There once was a student named Bessor
Whose knowledge grew lessor and lessor.
   It at last grew so small
   He knew nothing at all,
And today he's a college professor!

An assistant professor named Ddodd
Had manners arresting and odd.
   He said, "If you please,
   Spell my name with four 'd's.' "
Though one was sufficient for God.

A thoughtful young student at Lister
Went walking one day with his sister.
  When a bull at one poke
  Tossed her into an oak
It was weeks till the fond brother missed her.

Miss Fanny, a girl from Bryn Mawr,
Acquired a sleek, long-fyn cawr.
  Her control was superb
  Till she parked at a curb:
Then Fanny stuck out too dyrn fawr!

LOIS POWELL

An Oxford professor named Tring
Won the nickname of "God Save the King."
   For the kindliest hearted
   Of people departed
The moment he started to sing.

               PUNCH

Some instructors are blind as a mole.
Their notions of duty are droll.
   Severely one chid
   An innocent kid
For impulsively baring her sole.

Some varsity players, most brave,
A performance of "Hamlet" once gave.
   Said a wag, "Now let's see
   If it's Bacon or he—
That is, Shakespeare—who's turned in his grave."

Food and Drink

Said a sporty young person named Groat,
Who owned a black racehorse of note,
   "I consider it smart
   To dine à la carte,
But my horse always takes table d'oat."

Sighed a maiden both tender and true,
"I've done plenty of dreaming of you,
   For I'm in the habit
   Of eating Welsh rarebit
And there's no telling WHAT I will do!"

A half-baked tomato named Sue
Was tossed in to season a stew.
  She thoughtfully sighed
  As she simmered and fried,
"I'm damned if I don't—or I do."

There was a princess of Bengal
Whose mouth was exceedingly small.
  Said she, "It might be
  More simple for me
To do without eating at all."

There was an old man on the Rhine
Who was asked at what hour he'd dine.
  He replied, "At eleven,
  Four, six, three, and seven.
Not to mention a quarter to nine."

There was a young man so benighted
He didn't know when he was slighted.
  He went to a party
  And ate just as hearty
As if he'd been really invited.

FRANCES PARKINSON KEYES

A bibulous chap from Duquesne
Drank a whole jeraboam of champuesne.
   Said he with a laugh,
   As he quaffed the last quaff,
"I tried to get drunk, but in vuesne."

A ravenous gent in Japan
Ordered perishable fruit by the van.
   To the obvious question,
   "Won't you get indigestion?"
He replied, "What I can't eat, I can."

At a bistro, a chap named O'Reilly
Said, "I've heard these martinis praised heilly,
   But they're better by far
   At the neighboring bar
Where they're mixed much more smoothly and dreilly."

There was a young lady from Kent
Who said that she knew what it meant
   When men asked her to dine
   On caviar and wine.
She knew! How she knew! But she went!

    There once was a bonnie Scotch laddie
    Who said as he put on his plaidie:
       "I've just had a dish
       O' unco' guid fish."
    What HAD'e had? Had'e had haddie?

Miss Minnie McFinney, of Butte,
Fed always, and only, on frutte.
   Said she, "Let the coarse
   Eat of beef and of horse:
I'm a peach, and that's all there is tutte."

They tell of a hunter named Shephard
Who was eaten for lunch by a lephard.
   Said the lephard, "Egad!
   You'd be tastier, lad,
If you had been salted and pephard."

A gent with a drooping mustache
Chewed some hair out while eating his hache.
   The phrases profane
   That he shrieked in his pain
We shall represent here with a dache.

A shortage of cooks has produced
More kitchen-wise males than it used.
   Like that man of gal-LAN-try
   Who, leaving the pantry,
Remarked, "Well, MY cook has been goosed!"

There was a fair maid from Pomona.
The first time she ate a bologna
   She said, "It is queer
   And I really do fear
You must help me remove its kimono."

There was a young woman of Twickenham
Loved sausages—never got sick on 'em.
   She knelt on the sod
   And prayed to her God
To lengthen and strengthen and thicken 'em.

There was an old lady in Rye
Who was baked by mistake in a pie.
   To the household's disgust
   She emerged through the crust
And exclaimed, with a yawn, "Where am I?"

A certain young gourmet of Crediton
Took some pâté de foie gras and spread it on
   A chocolate biscuit,
   Then murmured, "I'll risk it."
His tomb bears the date that he said it on.

REV. CHARLES INGE

Yes, theirs was a love that was tidal
And it ended in cheer that was bridal.
  But the bridegroom said, "Dear,
  Let us please have some beer,"
And they buried them seidel by seidel.

A formidable gent from Taconic
Consumed vodka and rye like a tonic.
  But in his ninety-ninth year
  He swore off, for fear
(He said) that his thirst might grow chronic.

When you think of the hosts without no.
Who are slain by the deadly cuco.
  It's quite a mistake
  Of such food to partake:
It results in a permanent slo.

Girls

An Indian maiden, a Sioux,
As tempting as fresh honeydioux,
  Liked to show off her kneezes
  As she strolled past tepeezes,
And hear the braves holler, "Wioux! Wioux!"

Said a calendar model named Gloria,
"So the men can enjoy real euphoria,
  You pose as you are
  In Jan., Feb. and Mar.
Then in April they wanna see moria!"

A certain young lady named Hannah
Was caught in a flood in Montannah.
　　As she floated away,
　　Her beau, so they say,
Accompanied her on the piannah.

An old maid who came from Vancouver
Won a man with this adroit manouver:
　　She jumped on his knee
　　With a paean of glee
And now nothing on earth can remouver.

There once was a mlle.
With a form like a lovely glle.
　　The way that she laughed
　　Drove her suitors quite daughed
And they left her as angry as lle.

"I shall star," vowed a girl in Biloxi,
"By being Twentieth Century Foxi,"
    And her film career
    Really blossomed this year:
She's in charge of the mops at the Roxi.

There once lived a certain Miss Gale
Who turned most exceedingly pale,
    For a mouse climbed her leg
    (Don't repeat this, I beg),
And a splinter got caught in its tail.

A very young girl—call her Emma—
Was seized with a terrible tremma.
    She had swallowed a spider
    Which spun webs inside her.
Gadzooks, what an awful dilemma!

When she took that walk down the aisle
She was dressed in the latest of staisle,
    But a friend later said
    With a shake of her haid
That her petticoat hung down a maisle.

A damsel, seductive and handsome,
Got wedged in a sleeping room transom.
  When she offered much gold
  For release, she was told
That the view was worth more than the ransom.

OLIVER HERFORD

The ankle's chief end is exposiery
Of the latest designs in silk hosiery.
  Also, I suspect,
  It was made to connect
The part called the calf with the toesiery.

CAROLYN WELLS

An alluring young pig in Paree
Fills all of her suitors with glee,
  For when they implore
  Her to give a bit more
She invariably answers, "Wee, wee."

73

Said a fervent young lady of Hammels,
"I object to humanity's trammels!
   I want to be free!
   Like a bird! Like a bee!
Oh, why am I classed with the mammals?"

MORRIS BISHOP

A girl on a cruise boat named Mercer
Had a bit of a do with the purser.
   When people said, "Oh,"
   She agreed, "Yes, I know,
But the Captain was very much worser."

CAROLYN WELLS

There was a young maid in Tahiti
Whom the neighbors considered quite flahiti,
   For if Monday was fine
   You would find on her line
An extremely diaphanous nahiti.

A burleycue baby named Heath
Displayed what she wore underneath.
   But the morons who viewed her
   Thought she ought to be nuder
So she showed them the skin of her teeth.

A Birmingham miss named Rhoda
Maintained an immoral pagoda,
  Financed by wrecks
  Of the opposite sex
Who eventually couldn't affo'd her.

There once was a spinsterish lass
Who constructed her panties of brass.
   When asked, "Do they chafe?"
   She said, "Yes, but I'm safe
Against pinches, and snakes in the grass."

There was a young maid from Madras
Who had a magnificent ass;
  Not rounded and pink
  As you probably think—
It was gray, had long ears, and ate grass.

There was a young girl named Irene
Who was chosen as Stock Exchange queen,
　　For when in the mood
　　Was successfully wooed
By Merrill Lynch, Fenner and Beane.*

* Pierce and Smith were on vacation.

The Great and Near Great

In a notable family called Stein
There were Gertrude, and Ep, and then Ein.
　　Gert's writing was hazy,
　　Ep's statues were crazy,
And nobody understood Ein.

An early psychologist, Freud,
Had the bluenoses very anneud,
    Saying, "You cannot be rid
    Of the troublesome id,
So it might just as well be enjeud."

There was a composer named Liszt
Who from writing could seldom desiszt.
    He made Polonaise
    Quite worthy of praise,
And now that he's gone, he is miszt.

        Have you heard of Madam Lupescu?
        She came to Rumania's rescue.
            What a wonderful thing
            To buck up a king!
        Is democracy better? I esc you!

ROBERT K. HAAS

Mark Twain was a noteworthy male
Whose narratives sparkle like ale.
  And this Prince of the Grin
  Who once fathered Huck Finn
Can still hold the world by the tale.

A musician there was: Paderewski,
Who rarely would drink or would chewski.
  As a matinee blade
  He made Heifetz afraid
And quite broke the heart of John Drewski.

There was a great sculptor named Phidias
Whose knowledge of art was invidious.
  He carved Aphrodite
  Without any nightie,
Which outraged the purely fastidious.

When Cole Porter stopped off at Hong Kong
He composed a new national song.
  It was all in one note,
  This song that he wrote,
But it sounded superb on a gong.

History of a Sort

When thatte Saint George hadde slayen ye draggon,
He opened ye corke on a flaggon.
  And, wit ye welle,
  Within a short spelle
He had a bien plaisaunt olde jag on.

Said Nero to one of his train,
"Those Christians will surely refrain,
    Encased as they are
    In coatings of tar,
From burning my city again."

    Cleopatra, who thought they maligned her,
    Resolved there and then to be kinder.
        "If when pettish," she said,
        "I should chop off your head,
    Would you give me a gentle reminder?"

A columnist set out in quest
Of the source of an "original" jest.
    He found the remark
    Had been made in the Ark:
A discovery he's never confessed.

    A senator, Rex Asinorum,
    Was needed to make up a quorum.
        So he flew down from Venice,
        Asked, "Who knows where my pen is?"
    Then laconically scribbled, "I'm forum."

The fact is that Rome needed money
And, further, the Gauls got too funny.
  So they sent out some legions
  To clean up them regions.
J. Caesar? Yep, he was there, sonny.

That biblical villain named Cain
Was deceitful, perverse, and profane.
  With the leg of a table
  He conked Brother Abel
And hollered, "Remember the Maine!"

The great Aphrodite by Phidias
Once shocked Athens' ultra-fastidious.
  So some fussy old aunties
  Decked her out in lace panties—
Which made her look perfectly hideous.

When King Edward visited Warwick
He dwelled in a castle histarwick.
　On the damp castle mold
　He contracted a cold
And the doctor prescribed paregarwick.

A distinguished old king of Siam
Said, "For conquest I don't give a damn,
　But a maiden full grown
　Makes me leap from my throne.
They call me a bounder. I *am*."

When a train on the New York, New Ha
ven and Hartford went rolling one day
 Click clack down the track
 Without stopping or back
ing, the passengers fainted away.

ARTHUR W. DOBSON

There was a young man from Olean
Who invented a new submarine
 And one trembles to think,
 If he'd got it to sink,
What the fate of our fleet might have been!

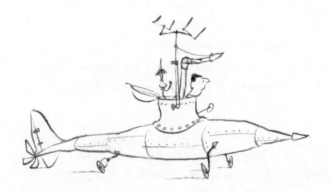

Human Foibles

Msgr. Ronald Knox, for a bet, induced a newspaper to print this classified advertisement:
 "An Anglican curate in want of a second-hand portable font, would exchange for the same a portrait (in frame) of the Bishop-elect of Vermont."

There was a young girl in the choir
Whose voice went up hoir and hoir,
 Till one Sunday night
 It vanished from sight
And turned up next day in the spoir.

He received from some thoughtful relations
A spittoon with superb decorations.
  When asked was he pleased,
  He grimaced and wheezed,
"It's beyond all my expectorations."

An incautious young man from Bay View
Carried all of his cash in a shiew.
  Along came a yegg
  And sawed off his legg
And escaped with a thousand or tiew.

A fellow named Crosby (not Bing)
Was asked by a hostess to sing.
  He replied, "Though it's odd,
  I can never tell 'God
Save the Weasel' from 'Pop Goes the King.' "

A senior at lunch in Purdue
Found quite a large mouse in his stew.
  Said the waiter, "Don't shout,
  And display it about,
Or the profs will be wanting one, too."

While humming Andante Cantabile
A sculptor constructed a mobile.
　　When it failed to revolve
　　He made this resolve:
"I really must build them more wobile."

A. C. SPECTORSKY

In the cloistered old town of Champaign
Lives a tall, very slender old jaign.
　　In her bathtub one night
　　She received *such* a fright
For she slid halfway down through the draign.

There was an old man of Tarentum
Who gnashed his false teeth till he bent 'em.
　　When they asked him the cost
　　Of what he had lost,
He replied, "I can't say, 'cause I rent 'em."

There was a young lady of Twickenham
Whose shoes were too tight to walk quick in 'em.
  She came back from a walk
  Looking whiter than chalk,
And took 'em both off and was sick in 'em.

OLIVER HERFORD

There once was a man of Calcutta
Who spoke with a terrible stutter.
  At breakfast he said,
  "Give me b-b-b-bread
And b-b-b-b-b-b-butter."

There was a young belle of old Natchez
Whose garments were always in patchez.
  When comment arose
  On the state of her clothes
She drawled, "When ah itchez, ah scratchez."

OGDEN NASH

There was a young damsel named Carol
Who liked to play stud for apparel.
  Her opponent's straight flush
  Brought a maidenly blush
And a hasty trip home in a barrel.

A lass who weighed many an oz.
Used words that nice girls don't pronoz.
   When a prankster unkind
   Yanked her chair from behind
Just to see, he explained, if she'd boz.

   There was a young lady from Lynn
   Who happened to sit on a pynn.
      But to add to her contour
      She'd stuck so much ontour,
   The point didn't puncture the skynn.

There was a young fellow of Perth
Who was born on the day of his birth.
   He was married, they say,
   On his wife's wedding day,
And he died when he quitted the earth.

There was an old man of Calcutta
Who coated his tonsils with butta,
   Thus converting his snore
   From a thunderous roar
To a soft, oleaginous mutta.

OGDEN NASH

There was a young lady named Shanker
Who dozed while a ship lay at anchor.
   She awoke in dismay
   When she heard the mate say,
"Let's hoist up the topsheet and spanker."

Our heroine fled to Bermuda
Where our villain forthwith pursued her.
   When he begged her, "Be mine,"
   And she answered him, "Nein,"*
Every man in the audience booed her.

* She was a German heroine.

A near-sighted spinster named Shite
Wore a pair of pajamas one night.
   As she happened to pass
   Near a large looking-glass
She exclaimed, "There's a man!" in delight.

Two eager and dashing young beaux
Were held up and robbed of their cleaux.
　　While the weather is hot
　　They won't mind a lot,
But what will they do when it sneaux?

There was a young girl of Asturias
Whose temper was frantic and furious.
　　She used to throw eggs
　　At her employer's legs—
A habit both costly and curious.

I once knew a gardener whose aunt
Sat down on his favorite plant.
　　He said, "Would you tell 'er
　　My feelings, old feller?
I've a wife and six kids, and I can't."

An inventive young man in Monroe
Built a weather-conditioned château.
    By his technical blunders
    The dining room thunders
And the bathrooms incessantly snow.

MORRIS BISHOP

A damsel at Vassar named Breeze
Weighed down with B.Lit.'s and D.D.'s
    Collapsed from the strain.
    Said her doctor, "It's plain
You are killing yourself—by degrees."

I once thought a lot of a friend
Who turned out to be in the end
    The southernmost part
    (As I'd feared from the start)
Of a horse with a northerly trend.

An accident really uncanny
Befell a respectable granny:
    She sat down in a chair
    While her false teeth were there
And bit herself right in the fanny.

There once was a fellow named Topping
Who fell down five flights without stopping.
 The janitor swore
 As the clunk hit the floor,
"It will take the whole afternoon mopping."

A mischievous miss from Woods Hole
Had a notion exceedingly droll:
 At a masquerade ball
 She wore nothing at all,
And backed in as a Parker House roll.

A prelate of very high station
Was impeached by a pious relation.
 He was found in a ditch
 With, I won't say a witch,
But a woman of no education.

JOHN WAYNE

Legalities

A chronic offender in Worcester
Told the court, "I'll not steal like I urcester."
    But he fell with a swoop
    On the first chicken coop
That he spied, and made off with a rucester.

A capricious young man in Mo.
Was determined to sit on a jo.
    But the judge called him down
    With a judicial frown
And the young man stalked out in a fo.

A newspaper writer named Fling
Could make copy from most anything.
 But the copy he wrote
 Of a ten-dollar note
Was so good he is now in Sing Sing.

  Some blue-nosed old censors one day
  Were required to pass on a play.
   They proclaimed, "If it's clever,
   Our answer is 'Never';
  If it puts folks to sleep, it can stay."

There was an old lawyer named Dolan
Whose income was happily swollen
 By charging big fees
 For interpreting these:
The , , the —, and the :

JOSEPH S. NEWMAN

Miscellaneous

The ladies inhabiting Venus
Have signaled us saying they've seen us.
    They add, "There's a yen here—
    For getting some men here—
And nothing but space is between us."

                          AL GRAHAM

There once was an African Mau-Mau
Who got into a rather bad row-row.
    The cause of the friction
    Was his practicing diction,
Saying, "How-how now-now brown-brown cow-cow."

A mayor who heartily laughed
When aughsked if he ever took graughed,
    Later sighed and denighed,
    "It's a matter of prighed,
But my cronies aughl think I am daughed."

95

I'd rather have fingers than toes;
I'd rather have ears than a nose;
   And as for my hair,
   I'm glad it's all there.
I'll be awfully sad when it goes.

GELETT BURGESS

      There was a faith healer of Deal
      Who said, "Although pain is not real,
         When I sit on a pin,
         And puncture my skin,
      I dislike what I fancy I feel."

When twins came, their father, Dan Dunn,
Gave "Edward" as name to each son.
   When folks said, "Absurd!"
   He replied, "Ain't you heard
That two Eds are better than one?"

BERTON BRALEY

Religion

There were two young ladies from Birmingham
And here is a story concerning 'em:
    They lifted the bib
    And tickled the rib
Of the bishop as he was confirming 'em.

A clergyman told from his text
How Samson was scissored and vexed.
    Then a barber arose
    From his sweet Sunday doze,
Got rattled, and shouted, "Who's next?"

There once was a boring young Rev.
Who preached till it seemed he would nev.
    His hearers, en masse,
    Got a pain at this pass,
And prayed—for relief of their neth.

There once was a pious young priest
Who lived almost wholly on yeast.
    "For," he said, "it is plain
    We must all rise again,
And I want to get started at least."

There was a young man who said, "Damn!
It is borne upon me that I am
    An engine which moves
    In predestinate grooves.
I'm not even a bus; I'm a tram!"

A modernist preacher of Redding
Pioneered with a parachute wedding.
    But the bride's wedding gown
    Just wouldn't stay down;
And you can't keep a cassock from spreading.

MORRIS BISHOP

There was a formidable student in Trinity
Who solved the square root of infinity.
   But it gave him such fidgets
   To count up the digits
That he chucked math and took up divinity.

There was a young fellow of Sherborne
Who attended his church in a turban.
   When they thumbed him outside
   He clearly implied
That he rated their ideas suburban.

There was a young man who said, "God,
It always has struck me as odd
   That the sycamore tree
   Simply ceases to be
When there's no one about in the quad."

School Days

A bright little lassie in Lawrence
Used language that came out in tawrence,
   Till informed by the teacher,
   "Your manners, dear creacher,
Are worse than your scholarship wawrence."

A pretty school mistress named Beauchamp
Said, "These monsters here, how can I teauchamp?
   For they will not behave
   Although I look grave
And in softest of tones I beseauchamp."

A father* once said to his son,
"The next time you get off a pun
   Get out in the yard
   And kick yourself—hard—
Then I'll pull it myself when you're done."

* No relation.

Some charming selections by Strauss
A pianist played at a school hauss.
　　The kids cried "Encore"
　　And clamored for more,
Though the teachers did nothing but grauss.

Sick, Sick, Sick!

A handsome young gent down in Fla.
Collapsed in a hospital ca.
　　A young nurse from Me.
　　Sought to banish his pe.
And shot him. Now what could be ha.?

There was a young man with a hernia
Who said to his doctor, "Gol dernia,
 When improving my middle,
 Be sure you don't fiddle
With matters that do not concernia."

HEYWOOD BROUN

Mr. Wimpfheimer rented a suite
In a building without any huite.
 He lived there six months
 But he never kicked onths
For a surgeon had cut off his fuite.

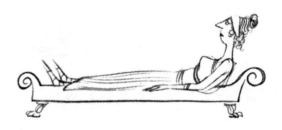

An Athenian gal—yes, a Greek—
Was deplorably skinny and weak.
 But her face turned deep red
 When her medico said,
"What you need is a good strong physeak."

There was a young gent in Laconia
Whose mother-in-law caught pneumonia.
   He hoped for the worst
   And just after May first
They buried her 'neath a begonia!

    There once were some learned M.D.'s
    Who captured some germs of disease
      And infected a train,
      Which, without causing pain,
    Allowed hundreds to catch it with ease.

OLIVER HERFORD

There was a young lady named Hannah
Who slipped on a peel of banannah.
   As she lay on her side
   More stars she espide
Than there are in the Star-Spangled Bannah.

    A railway official of Skewe
    Met an engine one day that he knew.
      Though he smiled and he bowed,
      That engine was proud
    And it cut him—yes, cut him in two!

Said a foolish young lady in Wales,
"A smell of escaped gas prevails."
    Then she searched with a light
    And later that night
Was collected—in seventeen pails.

LANGFORD REED

Said a lively young nurse out in Padua
To a visitor, "Please, sir, a dadua.
    I've come down for some pins
    For to wrap up the twins,
And to hear you remark, sir, how gladua."

Pour le Sport

There was an old person in Quorn
Who was sorry he'd ever been born.
    For some damnable hounds
    Chased a fox through his grounds
And entirely ruined his lawn.

At a bullfight in sunny Madrid
A tourist went clean off his lid.
   He made straight for a bull
   While the crowd yelled, "The fool
Will go home on a slab"—and he did.

There was a young lady of Wilts
Who walked all through Scotland on stilts.
   When they said, "Oh, how shocking
   To reveal so much stocking,"
She said, "How about *you* and your *kilts?*"

A golfer of sorts in Calcutta
Thought of curses too pungent to utter
   When his wife, as he found
   Ere commencing a round,
Was beating a rug with his putter.

While watching a game of croquet
A lady got caught in the wuet.
   She was struck in the eye
   By a ball that went beye
So she wears a glass orb to this duet.

There was a young fellow named Paul
Who attended a fancy dress ball.
   They say, just for fun,
   He dressed up as a bun,
And a dog ate him up in the hall.

A young beauty, an expert on skis,
Slalomed with a man who said, "Plis!
   On the next precipice
   Will you give me a kice?"
She said, "Quick! Before somebody sis!"

A gentleman sailor in Wales
Became expert at spitting in gales.
   He could spit in a jar
   From the top-gallant spar
Without even wetting the sails.

Bill Bounce, being fat for a jockey,
Tried steaming to make him less stocky.
  This heated him so
  That he had to eat snow,
And change his profession to hockey.

PAUL BARTLETT

A rascal far gone in lechery
Lured maids to their doom by his treachery.
  He invited them in
  For the purpose of sin
Though he said 'twas to look at his etchery.

A quiet young lady called Snookie
At betting was quite a smart cookie.
  Before every race
  She went home to her place
And curled up with a very good bookie.

In Iceland, a supple young miss
Enthused, "I think skating is bliss."
   This no more will she state
   For a slip of her skate

˙sıɥʇ ǝʞıʃ ƃuıɥʇǝɯos dn ƃuıpuǝ ɹǝɥ ʇɟǝ˥

Said the mate of a sailboat unique
To the cap'n, "What port shall we sique?"
   Said the cap'n, "We'll dock 'er
   In Davy Jones locker:
This blasted old tub's sprung a lique."

NEAR AND DISTANT PLACES

A Chinaman down in Ky.
Complained to a friend, "Me unly.
  The Southern chop suey
  Is how you say? Phooey?
And when they bring check I am sty."

There was a young girl from Nantucket
Who went down to Hell in a bucket.
  When she got there
  And they asked for her fare
She replied, "I propose that we ducket."

There was a young girl from St. Paul
Who wore a newspaper dress to a ball.
  But the dress caught on fire
  And burned her entire,
Front page—sporting section—and all.

A señora who strolled on the Corso
Displayed quite a lot of her torso.
  A crowd soon collected
  And no one objected
Though some were in favor of more so.

The food they now serve in Pekin
Made a once-buxom lady so thin
  That when she essayed
  To drink lemonade
She slipped through the straw and fell in.

There was an old monk in Siberia
Whose existence grew steadily drearier,
　　Till he broke from his cell
　　With a hell of a yell
And eloped with the Mother Superior.

A painter who came from Great Britain
Hailed a lady who sat with her knitain.
　　He remarked with a sigh,
　　"That park bench—well, I
Just painted it, right where you're sitain."

A lady from Atlanta, Ga.
Became quite a notable fa.
　　But she faded from view
　　With a quaint I.O.U.
That she signed, "Mrs. Lucrezia Ba."

A stripteaser named Cubbard in Kansas
Made a fortune by wiggling her Frances.
   When the censors got there
   Miss Cubbard was bare.
She explained, "I don't know where my fans is."

    There was a young man from Australia
    Who painted himself like a dahlia.
      The colors were bright,
      And the size was just right
    But the smell was a definite fahlia.

A daring young maid from Dubuque
Risked a rather decided rebuque,
   By receiving a prude
   In the absolute nude.
But he gasped, "If you only could cuque!"

    There are plenty of people in Md.
    Who think that their state is a fd.
      It seems odd to find
      That they don't really mind
    That Wis., not Md., is Dd.

A lady who rules Fort Montgomery
Says the wearing of clothes is mere mummery.
   She has frequently tea'd in
   The costume of Eden,
Appearing delightfully summery.

MORRIS BISHOP

A frisky young maiden in Glasgow
Gave a party that proved a fiasco.
   At ten-thirty, about,
   The lights all went out
Through a lapse on the part of the gas co.

The kings of Peru were the Incas,
Who got to be known as big drincas.
   They worshiped the sun
   And had lots of fun,
But the peasants all thought they were stincas.

A Chinaman touring the Nile
Said, "The Sphinx doesn't seem quite my style,
   But yonder there be
   Other ruins, I see,
And I'll pyramid those for a while."

FREDERICK VAN HORN

There was a young lady from Del.
Who was most undoubtedly wel.
   That to dress for a masque
   Wasn't much of a tasque,
But she cried, "What the heck will my fel.?"

There was a young fellow from Boise
Who at times was exceedingly noise.
   So his friends' joy increased
   When he moved way back east
To what people in Brooklyn called Joise.

JOHN STRALEY

There was a young lady from Guam
Who observed, "Now the sea is so calm,
    I'll swim out, for a lark,"
    But she met a large shark—
Let us now sing the Twenty-third Psalm!

There was a rich man of N.Y.
The gayest who ever dr. c.
    All manner of beasts
    Were observed at his feasts
But he never was known to ch. p.

There was a male dancer of Ipswich
Who took most astonishing skips, which
        So delighted a miss
        She demanded a kiss.
He replied, "On the cheek or the lips, which?"

A barber who lived in Moravia
Was renowned for his fearless behavia.
    An enormous baboon
    Broke into his saloon,
But he murmured, "I'm darned if I'll shavia."

A magician who came from Vt.
Sawed a woman in half for a stt.
 When she mildly asked whether
 He would put her together
He replied, "I've decided I wt."

A daring young fellow in Bangor
Sneaked a swift super-jet from its hangor.
 When he crashed in the bay
 Neighbors laid him away
In rather more sorrow than angor.

A lusty young wench in Toledo
Had a very inflated libido.
 When a couple of Finns
 Made her mother of twins
She just hollered with joy, "Oh, you keedo."

A man stopped his girl friend in Brussels
And charged, "You are wearing two bussels."
   She replied, "That's not true;
   It's a thing I don't do.
You are merely observing my mussels."

FUN WITH NAMES

There was a young fellow named Sidney,
Who drank till he ruined his kidney.
   It shrivelled and shrank
   As he sat there and drank,
But he had lots of fun doin' it, didney?

DON MARQUIS

A beautiful lady named Psyche
Is loved by a fellow named Yche.
   One thing about Ych
   The lady can't lych
Is his beard, which is dreadfully spyche.

A silly young fellow named Hyde
In a funeral procession was spied.
   When asked, "Who is dead?"
   He giggled and said,
"I don't know; I just came for the ride."

A farmer once called his cow "Zephyr";
She seemed such an amiable heifer.
  When the farmer drew near,
  She kicked off his ear,
Which made him considerably dephyr.

    A lovely young girl named Anne Heuser
    Declared that no man could surprise 'er.
      But a fellow named Gibbons
      Untied her Blue Ribbons
    And now she is sadder Budweiser.

A kindly old lady named Tweedle
Went to church and sat down on a needle.
  Though deeply imbedded,
  'Twas luckily threaded,
And was deftly pulled out by the beadle.

An amorous M.A.
Said of Cupid, The C.D.
  "From their prodigal use,
  He is, I deduce,
The John Jacob A.H."

TONGUE TWISTERS

A tutor who tooted a flute
Tried to teach two young tooters to toot.
  Said the two to the tutor,
  "Is it harder to toot, or
To tutor two tooters to toot?"

CAROLYN WELLS

There was a young person named Tate
Who went out to dine at 8:8,
  But I will not relate
  What that person named Tate
And his tête-à-tête ate at 8:8.

CAROLYN WELLS

She had pouted and protested, "Mr.!"
Because in the swing he had kr.
   And so for sheer spite
   On that very same night,
This Mr. kr. sr.

     A flea and a fly in a flue
     Were imprisoned so what could they do?
       Said the fly, "Let us flee,"
       Said the flea, "Let us fly,"
     So they flew through a flaw in the flue.

A canner, exceedingly canny,
One morning remarked to his granny,
   "A canner can can
   Anything that he can;
But a canner can't can a can, can he?"

CAROLYN WELLS

     A certain young chap named Bill Beebee
     Was in love with a lady named Phoebe.
       "But," he said, "I must see
       What the clerical fee
     Be before Phoebe be Phoebe Beebee."

There was an enchanting young bride
But from eating green apples she died.
  They soon had fermented
  Within the lamented
And made cider inside her inside.

"BEHEADED" LIMERICKS

A certain young pate who was addle
Rode a horse he alleged to be saddle.
   But his gust which was dis
   For his haps which were mis
Sent him back to his lack which was Cadil.

A budget I knew who was flutter
Lived the life of a fly which was butter.
   But ker which was po
   And girls that were show
Turned him into a snipe that was gutter.

A nice patch of golds that were mari
Belonged to a dan who was harri.
  When cals who were ras
  Filled their kets that were bas,
She put up a cade that was barri.

In Gonia once, which is Pata,
A clysm occurred that was cata:
  A gineer that was en
  Lost his ture that was den
In a torium there that was nata.

A chap was so pose that was adi,
And the butt of such nage that was badi,
  He solved that was re
  Not to lay that was de
In taking steps cal that were radi.

*Mrs. Arthur Shaw, of New Orleans, is the resource-
ful author of the five clever "beheaded limericks" in
this section—and if you think they're easy to invent,
just try one yourself!*